There's A Famine in the Land

Overcoming the World's Great Recession

Apostle Jacquelyn Hadnot, Thd.

There's A Famine in the Land

Published by Igniting the Fire Publishing
1314 North 38th Street
Kansas City, KS 66102
USA

Unless otherwise noted, scripture quotations are taken from the King James Version of the Bible with certain words changed to their modern equivalent; for example, "thee" and "thou" have been changed to "you, and "saith" has been changed to "say." Some words and punctuation marks have been modernized.

Certain ports of scriptures are italicized to emphasize a point that is made about that scripture.

Printed in the United States of America

Contents

There's A Famine in the Land

Introduction

IF my people which are called by My Name...
Do we really know who we are? Do we know
whose we are? I was born Jacquelyn Brown, that
means I know who my earthly father and mother
are. Beyond that I am child of the King of Kings
and Lord of Lords. That also means I know who
my heavenly father is. It means that I can call on
Him and He will answer me. It also means that
He knows the thoughts and plans for my life. He
knows the directions I should take. His will for
my life was set before the foundation of the
world.

He knows the plans for our nation and the people
that dwell within. Why is it that we don't seek
His advice? Why don't we allow our Holy and

Sovereign Lord to govern our nation? Why have we allowed the enemy to manipulate our government, our educational system, even our churches? Why have we taken the bait of Satan and removed the hand of the Lord from the very fiber of our society? Why have we allowed the enemy to rob us of our destiny as a great nation?

Are we headed for spiritual and civil unrest? Are we headed towards a famine from which we might never recover? Are we headed down a road of massive destructive proportions?

This book started out as a short essay given to me by the Lord at 3 a.m. Out of obedience, I began writing, not sure what He would do with it, but certain that it was a cry to His people for change.

We must, as a people turn our faces and hearts back towards God. *"If My people who are called by My name humble themselves and pray and seek My face and turn from their wicked ways, then I will hear from heaven, will forgive their sin and will heal their* land (2 Chronicles 7:14) and *then I will rebuke the devourer for you"* (Malachi 3:11).

Take this short journey with me and discover what the Lord is saying regarding a time in history where we have entered the worst recession since the great depression of the 1930's.

There is a remnant that God is going to shine through, a remnant that has not bowed to the Baal's of this world's system. A remnant is still standing firm as people that God has chosen show a dying world that He is still blessing that which belongs to Him.

There's A Famine in the Land

Chapter 1

The Great Recession:
There's A Famine in the Land

Recently, the Lord spoke to my heart and said, *"There is a famine coming and it must come if the people are to hear Me. Famine for food, water and the Word. This is just the beginning, it will get worse. Prepare, prepare, prepare. I am pulling the covers back to expose the filthy things being done in the church in order to turn the people back to Me. They worship man. Leaders have become idols in an idolatrous society - it is in the church. A cry must go out that there is a great intensity from the enemy like never before. Warn the people to beware, lest they be deceived."* It has been a while since the Lord spoke the warning about the famine that is headed our way. Thus the need for this book. I must be obedient and warn the people about the famine in the land. Some individuals are crying *prosperity is on the way* or *money is coming.* Both of these may be true, but let's look at the current economic picture as it stands in this decade.

In the last three years hundreds of thousands of jobs have been lost due to a dwindling economy. Hundreds of thousands of families have been displaced from their homes. Churches by the thousands are being foreclosed on and the sheep are being scattered. Schools are shutting down and children are being herded together like cattle into overcrowded schools.

The government tells us that the unemployment rate is 10%, when in fact, if they were to factor in the underemployed, individuals that stopped looking for work, and individuals that are no longer eligible for unemployment benefits, the unemployment rate would hover around 16 to 17%. A staggering number to say the least.

Spending by our government has ballooned out of control. The rate of spending on the federal government level is staggering. We have gone from spending approximately $300 billion per year on national defense to spending in excess of $640 billion.

We are indebted to foreign countries that loathe us. We have accumulated debt that exceeds three trillion dollars. We have borrowed more than we can ever repay. In fact, the debt we have accumulated over the past years will never be repaid in our lifetime. We have accumulated debt that the next generation will inherit. What an inheritance to leave your children? A debt that they can never repay.

We owe foreign countries such as China, Russia, United Kingdom, Brazil, Hong Kong and Japan. We have borrowed money from these countries in order to pay our bills. This has placed our debt ratio in an alarmingly high position. For this reason, the United States will not play a major role in the end time's economic system. Individuals that once held strong retirement plans have lost over $2 trillion between 2007 and 2008. What is happening to our economy?

The federal government is running a deficit monthly and we are hemorrhaging money at a pace our tax contributions cannot absorb. The only solution we are offered from our governmental leaders is to increase taxes. Tax increases on the local, state and federal level are steadily on the rise. Not on any level can they justify putting such an additional burden on the backs on the people. They cannot justify taxing the few remaining employed individuals while so many more are out of work. Could this be a sign of the coming failure of our economic system?

Spending on the state level is even worse. Chris Christie, governor of New Jersey spoke in a 60 Minutes interview about the condition of our economy from the state level. When asked if the economic conditions were wide spread. He answered, *"Yes, of course it is. It's not like you could avoid it forever. Because it's here now and the federal government doesn't have the money any more to paper over it for the states. The day of reckoning has arrived, that's it and it's going to arrive everywhere. Time may vary a little bit depending on which state you're in, but its coming* (60 Minutes Interview, December 2010).

I believe that within the next two years we are going to see severe changes in the way federal and state entitlement or social programs are distributed. Programs such as welfare, SSI, Medicaid, Medicare, food stamps and the like. Changes that will deeply affect the underprivileged like never before. Entitlement programs will suffer and with that we will see a severe increase in crime. I believe that in the next few years, we will sit by and watch as entitlement programs such as welfare are discontinued because the state piggy banks are dwindling at an alarming rate. What will happen when this happens? Families that rely on state assistance will suffer, crime will increase and our countries infrastructure will witness another deadly blow. Our country can no longer provide the most basic of needs for it's poor and destitute. The Lord said that He was sending a famine that includes food. I can speak from first hand experience that the famine for food has arrived.

Weekly, we feed families in record numbers at It Is Written Ministries. Our numbers as of 2010 have more than doubled. Several food pantries in Kansas City have closed their doors while others are running out of food on a regular basis.

Families are struggling to feed their children, struggling to clothe their families and struggling to make ends meet. A cut in entitlement programs will mean an increase in the need for more financial and food assistance. *He who gives to the poor will never want, But he who shuts his eyes will have many curses* (Proverbs 28:27).

The gap between the *haves* and the *have not's* has grown at an enormous rate. The *great economic divide* has no color preference, no gender qualifications, no ethic associations, and no class differentials. The *"economic divide"* has affected every corner of American life. The working poor are in every city and state, every race, creed and color. The Great Recession is no respecter of persons. Individuals that came to this country with hopes of living the American dream are quickly realizing that the American dream has dimmed. They too have become victims of the "Great Recession."

There have been approximately twelve recessions since the "Great Depression" of the 1930's (which lasted four years and 7 months), but this is by far the worse recession we have had to endure. And endure we must, because our government has turned its back on God. Our schools have turned their backs on God. And even some of our churches have turned their backs on God.

Why would a sovereign God bless something that He has no part in? Why would our Holy God condone a system that places a yoke of bondage on the backs of its people? Why would a righteous God uphold that which is unrighteous? Why would a jealous God allow the worship of other gods? Our God is holy, righteous, jealous - omniscient, omnipresent and omnipotent. Therefore, He sees all, is all and is everywhere. The Almighty Jehovah God saw the current events coming and allowed it to happen. Why? Let's revisit His statement, *"There is a famine coming and it must come if the people are to hear Me. Famine for food, water and the Word. This is just the beginning, it will get worse. Prepare, prepare, prepare. I am pulling the covers back to expose the filthy things being done in the church in order to turn the people back to Me. They worship man. Leaders have become idols in an idolatrous society - it is in the church. A cry must go out that there is a great intensity from the enemy like never before. Warn the people to beware, lest they be deceived."*

He must allow the famine because the people will not listen. Who are the people? The government, school officials, churches, individuals - the world. The Bible states in II Chronicles 7:14: *if My people who are called by My name humble themselves and pray and seek My face and turn from their wicked ways, then I will hear from heaven, will forgive their sin and will heal their land. "Now My eyes will be open and My ears attentive to the prayer offered in this place. "For now I have chosen and consecrated this house that My name may be there forever, and My eyes and My heart will be there perpetually.*

We all belong to God, but we are not all proclaiming His name. Unfortunately, many individuals have turned their backs on God. Many have walked away (fallen away) from Him and have begun serving other gods. The money we once trusted in has let us down. Individuals trust in 401Ks, stocks, bonds and the like. The rate of municipal bond defaults will begin to surface within the next year. According to Meredith Whitney a Wall Street analyst, "as many as 50 to 100 municipal bonds will begin to default with the next twelve months which will amount to hundreds of millions of dollars lost. *(60 Minutes Interview 12/19/2010).*

Agencies like Standard and Poors miscalculated the housing collapse. They are now saying don't worry about anything the bond issue will be fine. However, according to Ms Whitney there is something to worry about and it will begin within the next twelve months.

I am putting my trust in God who is trying to warn us about the impending financial calamity that is knocking at our door. I will not believe the report of the government because their reckless spending, financial irrresponsibilities, lies, schemes and gimmicks to hide the true picture from the public are what have gotten us into this mess.

Our government is a godless government that

demands money from the people like pimps demand money from prostitutes. Daily the government is whoring out the people and a-whoring after other gods. *My people [habitually] ask counsel of their [senseless] wood [idols], and their staff [of wood] gives them oracles and instructs them. For the spirit of harlotry has led them astray and they have played the harlot, withdrawing themselves from subjection to their God* (Hosea 4:12 AMP).

As a nation we are seeking the advice from everyone EXCEPT our Lord and Savior. We ask the government for help with the churches and ministries that God births through us. Subjecting the ministries to the yoke of the government through grants and the like. We have allowed the government to tax us without representation. They spend the tax dollars on godless research, condone abortion spending, and validate same sex marriages, refuse to sanction the pornography industry, while in the same breath allowing senior citizens to suffer, cutting spending on education and turning a deaf ear to the plight of the homeless. Why would God bless the government when it embraces everything He is against?

We have surrendered our rights of freedom to a task master who is relentless in his pursuit of greater gain - our personal economic status will suffer. Our economic system is just the beginning, if left unchecked the freedom to worship will be the next thing the government tries to control.

The Bible warns us in Hosea 4:14: *"That the people without understanding shall stumble and fall and come to ruin."* As a nation we are on the brink of ruin? It is evident that our economic structure has stumbled and is on the brink of bankruptcy.

Bankruptcy is a word that I thought I would not utter in regards to the solvency of the United States of America. But it is possible and it is closer than we realize. We are squandering our way into bankruptcy. At the rate we are incurring debt on every governmental level, I believe that local and state governments will be the first to crumble under the weight of its debt. We will begin to see cities and states begin to declare bankruptcy at an alarming rate.

Because we have allowed out of control spending, godless investments and uncontrolled greed in our business community we are in a sense being carried away captive by our godless pursuits. Pursuits of money, fortune and fame have left us morally and financially bankrupt.

Money making schemes are on the rise because the "spirit of mammon" has taken control and as a result, it has fanned the fire of moral, spiritual and financial bankruptcy. The church has now entered its own form of bankruptcy or depression.

Chapter 2

The Great Church Depression

Our society has allowed money to lead us astray and carry us away captive. The church cannot be excused from this either. We have built bigger buildings that have placed a yoke of bondage on the backs of the congregation. The day the doors opened and the "mega-church" emerged was the day that the yokes of bondage were dispersed. Elder John built a 10,000 seat mega-church, so Elder Mike needed to build a 15,000 seat facility. It set off a chain reaction and 30 other pastors built huge facilities - only to discover that in a dwindling economy, people stop giving. When the tithes and offering dry up the bank notes become delinquent. When the bank note is delinquent six months or more, the bank will begin foreclosure proceedings. When foreclosure happens people are displaced.

When the people are displaced the sheep will scatter.

According to the U.S. Census, spending on construction of **houses of worship** had almost doubled from $3.8 billion in 1997 to $6.2 billion in 2007. Now, experts claim that they are seeing more stress in churches than they have in modern history. A review of foreclosure filings in the Thomson Reuters Westlaw legal database shows proceedings against American churches have almost tripled since December of 2007, when the crisis had first began. Like struggling homeowners who are suffering, this may also be the *great church depression.*

(Loansafe.org)

A new book, "The State of Church Giving," says congregations have waning influence among charitable causes because their focus now seems to be on institutional maintenance rather than spreading the gospel and healing the world. It also found a dip in money given to churches during the 2008 recession, even while donations to religious organizations overall increased.

- Giving to churches declined to 2.4 percent of a donor's income, lower than during the first years of the Great Depression; an additional $172 billion could be available if church members tithed 10 percent.

- Church giving spent on "benevolence" including global missions and social services slipped to 0.35 percent of income, the lowest in the study's 40-year sample. Giving for "congregational finances" including staff salaries and building maintenance was at 2 percent; roughly steady for the previous 20 years.

- While charitable giving nationwide fell 10.6 percent from 2007 to 2008, donations to "church, religious organizations" increased 6.5 percent, according to the U.S. Bureau of Labor Statistics.

Matt Vande Bunte | The Grand Rapids Press

Pastors will need to be honest with their congregations and with themselves about this economic crisis. This is the time that we must all come together. (Loansafe.org).

I have never understood the need for the "mega-church" because it appears that we are warehousing people. We should be building the Kingdom of God and not building bigger buildings. We should not be warehousing people Sunday after Sunday. Whatever happened to "the equipping of the saints?" The Bible tells us to "go ye..." Whatever happened to go ye into all nations? What would happen if on any given Sunday we packed up the church buses and went out into the streets and told someone about Jesus? What would happen if the church missionaries prepared meals and went on the mission field under the bridges and fed the homeless? What would happen if the deacons walked the streets and told the lost young men on the streets selling drugs about a living Savior that wants to show them a better way? What would happen if the women of the church embraced the young girls giving their bodies away and told them that Jesus loves them and wants to give them a better life? I believe the churches would be full of people hungry for God and a better way of life.

There is enough of the Word of God in 70% of the pew huggers that they are equipped to go out and tell a dying world about a living Savior. What would happen if the pastors of the "mega-churches" of 5,000+ would take associate pastors or ministers that are under his charge and send each one out with 500 to 1000 people and start a church on the other side of town? I believe the Lord would give the increase in each church, ministry and community by bringing in the lost souls. **Have we forgotten that souls are at stake?** And I am not talking about the souls that sit in the pew every Sunday stuffed like a fat rat on the word of God. Never redistributing the word they freely received. The pastors charge is to feed the sheep, the sheep should in turn share the Word with a least one person a week.

The Bible warns us that the Lord is tired of our whorish ways: *"Because I am broken with their whorish heart, which hath departed from me, and with their eyes, which go a-whoring after their idols: and they shall loathe themselves for the evils which they have committed in all their abominations" (Ezekiel 6:9).*

Unfortunately, many church goers are too busy trying to make a name, striving for power and position in the church or looking for the hook up, that we fail to see the enemy creeping in. We fail to see that we are not fulfilling the great commission and therefore, we are being disobedient to the charge given to us by Christ Jesus. Is this why the church is not growing?

Have we forgotten that are called to serve the Lord? Are we serving God or man? Who are we serving?

Chapter 3

Who Are We Serving?

As a nation we are not growing. As a people we are not growing. As the church we are not growing. Because we have heaped to ourselves the pleasures of this world, God is broken because of the things we have done. That is why there is a famine in the land. We cannot serve God and money. We cannot serve God and fame. We cannot serve God and the rudiments and doctrines of this world.

We have left ourselves vulnerable to the attacks of Satan. We have allowed the enemy to infiltrate our homes, school, government, and even our churches. We have opened the doors and given Satan free reign over the most important areas of our lives. *"See to it that no one takes you captive through philosophy and empty deception, according to the tradition of men, according to the elementary principles of the world, rather than according to Christ"* (Colossians 2:8.) We have been taken captive through empty promises, watered down messages and traditions that are not found in the Word of God.

We have voted for politicians that were ungodly, pledged our allegiance to the television celebrities and chewed on milk toast proclaiming it is the Word of God. We have been lead astray by false prophets and false teachers simply because they carry a big following. We have become so captivated by the faces on television that we have forgotten to check the fruit. Jesus said in John 7:24, *"Stop judging by mere appearances, and make a right judgment."*

There's A Famine in the Land

Unfortunately, many church attendees stopped taking a Bible to church and now rely on the pastor to tell them what is in the Bible. When this happened a spirit of laziness crept in and people no longer seek after the Word of God for themselves.

When the government began to slither his hand into the business affairs of the church, we allowed them to tell us what to preach and how to preach it. The church became afraid to address issues such as homosexuality for fear of prosecution. That was the day when the government crept into the church and hindered the true work of the cross. Which is to bring the people to repentance and lead them to salvation? When we continually allow the hands of the ungodly into the church, we are opening doors that precipitate the rise of ungodliness in the

There's A Famine in the Land

church.

Chapter 4
The Rise of Wickedness in the Church

Because we have turned our faces away from God as a people, as a nation, as the world - wickedness is erupting everywhere. We have become a lawless people in a lawless society. Yes, we have the law of the land, but what about the laws of God? When we allowed the government to take God out of every area, we opened the doors to civil and spiritual unrest. Civil unrest because our social structure is crumbling around us as people are homeless, hopeless and helpless to defend themselves from poverty, crime and illness. Spiritual unrest as people begin to fall away from the church. While others challenge the Bible as the inspired Word of God.

There's A Famine in the Land

Each week the doors of the church open and fewer people are walking through the doors. For many that attend church, the reverential fear of the Lord is gone. Individuals attend church on Sunday, but gamble, cheat, steal, commit whoredoms or murder on Monday. It is not just the congregation, some of the filthy things being done are from leaders in the church. Look at what God showed Ezekiel: *And He said to me, "Son of man, do you see what they are doing, the great abominations which the house of Israel are committing here, so that I would be far from My sanctuary? But yet you will see still greater abominations." Then He brought me to the entrance of the court, and when I looked, behold, a hole in the wall. He said to me, "Son of man, now dig through the wall." So I dug through the wall, and behold, an entrance. And He said to me, "Go in and see the wicked abominations that they are committing here." So I entered and looked, and behold, every form of creeping things and beasts and detestable things, with all the idols of the house of Israel, were carved on the wall all around. Standing in front of them were seventy elders of the house of Israel, with Jaazaniah the son of Shaphan standing among them, each man with his censer in his hand and the fragrance of the cloud of incense rising. Then He said to me, "Son of man, do you see what the elders of the house of Israel are committing in the dark, each man in the room of his carved images? For they say, 'The LORD does not see us; the LORD has forsaken the land.' "And He said to me, "Yet you will see still greater abominations which they are committing." Then He brought me to the entrance of the gate of the LORD'S house which was toward the north; and behold, women were sitting there weeping for Tammuz. He said to me, "Do you see this, son of man? Yet you will see still greater abominations than these." Then He brought me into the inner court of the LORD'S house. And behold, at the entrance to the temple of the LORD, between the porch and the altar, were about twenty-five men with their backs to the temple of the LORD and their faces toward the east; and they were prostrating themselves eastward toward the sun. He said to me, "Do you see this, son of man? Is it too light a thing for the house of Judah to commit the abominations which they have committed here, that they have filled the land with violence and provoked Me repeatedly? For behold, they are putting the twig to their nose. "Therefore, I indeed will deal in wrath. My eye will have no pity nor will I spare; and though they cry in My ears with a loud voice, yet I will not listen to them"* (Ezekiel 8:6-18).

The actions of a fallen people can be seen in these passages from Ezekiel.

1. Because so much filth is going on in the church the Lord said, the great abominations which are committed, are driving Him from His sanctuary?

2. We have allowed wickedness, filth and perversion into the House of God - *every form of creeping things and beasts and detestable things, with all the idols were carved on the wall all around.* There are churches with stained glassed windows that carry the carvings of the Masonic Order, the Illuminati and other cult practices. How can this happen

in a house that calls itself a house of God?

3. The enemy has deceived the world into believing that the Lord cannot see or does not care what is going on in the world or in the church *...each man in the room of his carved images? For they say, 'The LORD does not see us; the LORD has forsaken the land.'*

4. People are serving other gods: *women were sitting there weeping for Tammuz.* (Tammuz was an idol god which the people worshipped.)

5. Man began to worship not only other gods, but also the sun - *at the entrance to the temple of the LORD, between the porch and the altar, were about twenty-five men with their backs to the temple of the LORD and their faces toward the east; and they were prostrating*

themselves eastward toward the sun.

6. Are we taking God Almighty too lightly? Are we saying to a Holy God, Maker of heaven and earth that He can't or won't do anything to us? *Is it too light a thing for the house of Judah to commit the abominations which they have committed here, that they have filled the land with violence and provoked Me repeatedly?*

7. It's no wonder the Lord has turned us over to our own devices - government, schools, churches, etc. *and though they cry in My ears with a loud voice, yet I will not listen to them."*

God warned Ezekiel three times, *"Yet you will see still greater abominations than these."* With each passing day we are seeing greater abominations in our schools, churches, work places, nation - all around the world. Religious persecution is on the rise in every corner of the world. We read about the atrocities in other countries, often thinking it could never happen in the United States, but I beg to differ. Religious persecution is slowly creeping it's way into the very fabric of our religious freedom.

We say that we love God and yet as nation, as a people, even as the church we have forsaken our first love. God gives us this declaration in Isaiah 58: *"Yet they seek Me day by day and delight to know My ways, As a nation that has done righteousness And has not forsaken the ordinance of their God. They ask Me for just decisions, They delight in the nearness of God"* (Isaiah 58:2).

There's A Famine in the Land

We ask God for help with our finances, marriages, employment, but when was the last time we just asked Him for His presence? We delight in going to church on Sunday, but when was the last time we went just to experience His manifested presence?

We say that as a nation we are righteous simply because "In God We Trust" is engraved on our money. "In God We Trust" is on our money, but is it in our hearts? "In God We Trust" is on our money, but is He in our school system?

"In God We Trust" is on our money, but is He in our government and decision making process?

"In God We Trust" is on our money, but is it in our churches? Where is your God? Who is your God?

There's A Famine in the Land

With everything that has been written, it leads me to the topic of this book: The Great Recession: There's a famine in the land. Do you not see it? Can you not recognize it?

Chapter 5
The Great Recession

Looking back at the opening statement, *"The famine must come if the people are to hear."* Because we are not listening to God and following His direction, He has allowed *"The Great Recession"* to hit the world. It not only hit the United States, but other countries as well. It has affected the United Kingdom, Japan, Ireland, China and many others.

Here is the definition of *recession:*

In economics, a **recession** is a business cycle contraction, a general slowdown in economic activity over a period of time for more than two consecutive quarters. During recessions, many macroeconomic indicators vary in a similar way. Production, as measured by Gross Domestic Product (GDP), employment, investment spending, capacity utilization, household incomes, business profits and inflation all fall during recessions; while bankruptcies and the unemployment rate rise.

Recessions generally occur when there is a widespread drop in spending often following an adverse supply shock or the bursting of an economic bubble. Governments usually respond to recessions by adopting expansionary macroeconomic policies, such as increasing money supply, increasing government spending and decreasing taxation. (wikipedia.org)

The unemployment rate of US grew to 8.5

percent in March 2009 (currently around 10.2 percent), and there have been 5.1 million job losses as of March 2009 since the recession began in December 2007. That is about five million more people unemployed compared to a year ago. This has become the largest annual jump in the number of unemployed persons since the 1940s. Has anyone asked the question, how many of the millions of unemployed, underemployed and disenfranchised workers are church members? How many have been displaced from their homes? When will it all end?

As I stated earlier there have been twelve recessions since the *Great Depression* which lasted from August 1929 to 1933. Look at the list of recessions that have occurred over the years.

There's A Famine in the Land

List of Recessions

1. Recession of 1937
2. Recession of 1945
3. Recession of 1949
4. Recession of 1953
5. Recession of 1958
6. Recession of 1960-61
7. Recession of 1969–70
8. Recession of 1973 - 1975
9. Recession of 1980 - Jan - July 1980
10. Recession of <u>Early 1980s</u>, 1981-82
11. Recession of <u>Early 1990s</u> July 90–Mar 91
12. Recession of <u>Early 2000s</u> Mar 01–Nov 2001

I included this information because the Bible tells us that people perish for lack of knowledge and I believe knowledge is power. Again, there have been twelve recessions since the Great

There's A Famine in the Land

Depression and when we began the Great Recession in December of 2007, we had no idea of the devastating effects it would have on us as a country and as a people. The effects of this recession have shaken the very fiber of our being. It has shaken our financial base: governmental, individual and church. It has challenged the very core of our existence: governmental, individual and church. In other words, it has caused a sickness in the land. There is sickness in the land and there is sin in the camp. *"If my people, who are called by my name, will humble themselves and pray and seek my face and turn from their wicked ways, then will I hear from heaven and will forgive their sin and will heal their land"* (2 Chronicles 7:14).

We must turn our faces and our hearts back to God. We must turn our schools, government, churches, homes and families back to God. We must surrender ALL to God and His mighty hand over our lives. We must stop being as the children of Israel, when having heard rebelled.

God is speaking to us with conditions that must be met if He is to heal our land. God is not in the business of compromising with us. He said, be holy for He is holy. Holiness is not an option.

IF

- ➤ He said: IF my people - are we His people?

- ➤ He said *which are called by My name* - do we call ourselves children of God?

- ➤ He said, *will humble ourselves and pray* - are we a nation that prays? Are we praying people? Are we a church that is praying?

- ➤ He said, *seek My face* - are we seeking the

face of God or the hand of God?

➢ He said, *turn from our wicked ways* - Have we repented of our sins? Have we changed our mindset about our sins and see them as our Holy God sees them: wicked and detestable?

THEN

➢ God said He will honor his promise after we have met the conditions: *then will I hear from heaven and will forgive their sin and will heal their land.*

When we meet the conditions God has set forth in His Word, His eyes will be open and His ears attentive to the prayers offered in our government, our schools, our homes and our churches. We MUST get back to the basics: God is ALL and in ALL. Remember, judgment begins at the House of God.

God is and has always been an integral part of the very fiber of our nation. Just take a look at the Preamble to the Declaration of Independence.

*We hold these truths to be self-evident, that all men are created equal, that they are endowed, by their **Creator**, with certain unalienable rights, that among these are Life, Liberty, and the pursuit of Happiness.*

Also look at The Pledge of Allegiance:

*"I pledge allegiance to the Flag of the United States of America, and to the Republic for which it stands, **one Nation under God**, indivisible, with liberty and*

justice for all."

The Pledge of Allegiance was first published for Columbus Day, on September 8, 1892, in the Boston magazine *The Youth's Companion*. It was written by a member of the magazine's staff, Francis Bellamy. The publication of the Pledge and its wide redistribution to schools in pamphlet form later that year lead to a recitation by millions of school children, starting a tradition that continues today. Congress recognized the Pledge officially in 1942, and in 1954 added the phrase "under God" to the text. In 1943, the Supreme Court overturned *Gobitis* and ruled in its *Barnette* decision (319 US 624) that school children could not be forced to recite the Pledge as a part of their school day routine. (U.S. Constitution Online).

There's A Famine in the Land

Even in the most basic writings of our government, God has always been there. With the advancement of the atheist movements and the ACLU, we are allowing a hand full of individuals to remove God from the face of our pledge of allegiance to God. Our schools, jobs, government and even our churches are failing because we have failed to pledge allegiance to our Holy God. It's no wonder we are in a recession. A recession for food: spiritual and natural.

Chapter 6
Can We Turn it Around?

We have placed too much dependence on man and money and not enough dependence on God. Trusting in God means, "I don't care what tomorrow holds, because God holds my tomorrow." Yes, we are in a recession. Yes, money is tight - in fact it is too tight to mention. Yes, the situation looks dark, but Jesus is the Light of the world. It's time to turn it around...

We have placed too much emphasis on money and the things that money can buy. God sees money in a way that is totally opposite from our point of view. His concern is not the massive storehouses of wealth we have accumulated or the bling-bling we flaunt so bodaciously. God is concerned with what we store up in heaven. He desires that our financial prosperity be in alignment with our soul's prosperity. *"Beloved, I pray that in all respects you may prosper and be in good health, just as your soul prospers"* (3 John 1:2).

We are warned by the Apostle Paul in 1 Timothy 6:17 not to put our trust in the wealth of this world: *"Instruct those who are rich in this present world not to be conceited or to fix their hope on the uncertainty of riches, but on God, who richly supplies us with all things to enjoy."*

When we store up money and other earthly gain without any consideration for our spiritual gain, we are allowing the enemy to deceive us and rob us of our spiritual inheritance. Do not store up for yourselves treasures on earth, where moth and rust destroy, and where thieves break in and steal.

"But store up for yourselves treasures in heaven, where neither moth nor rust destroys, and where thieves do not break in or steal; for where your treasure is, there your heart will be also (Matthew 6:19-21).

Second Chronicles 7:14 tells us to seek... Matthew 6:33 tells us to seek... By combining the two scriptures we get a clear picture of the command God is placing before us.

If my people, who are called by my name, will humble themselves and pray and seek my face and turn from their wicked ways, then will I hear from heaven and will forgive their sin and will heal their land. And if you will seek (aim at and strive after) first of all MY kingdom and MY righteousness (MY way of doing and being right), and then all these things taken together will be given you besides. (Paraphrased).

Can we turn it around? Yes, we can by turning around our lives, our hearts and our country back to God. Before we can turn to God we must first turn from something or someone. As the Lord leads, here are some things we can do to turn things around. There are things we MUST turn TO and things we MUST turn FROM.

1. As a nation we must **turn from** wickedness and the practice of being anti-God.

2. As a people we must **turn from** our wicked ways and sinful practices and **turn** our hearts backs **to God**.

3. We must set the house in order by becoming a praying church, removing the money changers from the house of God, destroying the yokes of bondages we have placed on the people, returning to true ministry of helping the widows, orphans, homeless and others.

4. We must abolish the idols we have erected in the church: idols of money, fame, position and titles.

5. We must tear down the denominational walls that divide the people and keep us segregated.

6. We must come together and help other churches or ministries that are struggling and band together to show the world that "*as for me and my house, we will serve the Lord.*"

7. We must stop allowing the government to

whore out churches and ministries by pooling our resources to build the Kingdom of God.

8. We must leave the anti-Christian doctrines behind and adopt a stance of holding a "blood stained" banner that carries the blood of Jesus.

9. We must not allow the enemy to come in through deceptive devices that attract people, but don't save souls.

10. We must once again preach the cross of Christ and the message of salvation.

11. We must denounce publicly any teachings that are not the teachings of the uncompromising Word of God.

12. We must preach Jesus and Him crucified.

13. We must come from behind the walls of the

church and reach the homeless, drug addicts, prostitutes, unemployed, disenfranchised, incarcerated, and elderly and the sick.

14. We must not shut up, shut down, hold back or turn back.

15. We must stand on the strength of God's Word.

16. We must preach an uncompromising message to a compromising world.

17. We must make the gospel of Jesus Christ available to everyone who desires it - without regard to the cost.

18. We must be good stewards of all that God entrusts us with.

19. We must not walk in fear of what the world says about us or tries to do to us.

20. We must trust in the Lord with all our heart and lean not on our own understanding, but in all our ways we must acknowledge the Lord and allow Him to direct our paths.

21. We must show the world the love of Christ and we must spread that love to all we meet.

22. We must not be conformed to this world, but we must be transformed by the renewing of our minds.

23. We must present ourselves to God as living sacrifices being holy to Him.

24. We must allow prayer back in our schools, our government and work places.

25. We must end the denominational segregation that has stunted the growth of our churches.

26. We must get back to the heart of worship and remove entertainment from the church.

Let's face it, the Great Recession is here and it will be here for a while. We must begin to look at our situation and seek the Lord for ways to weather the storm of the Great Recession. King David said it best, *"I have been young and now I am old, Yet I have not seen the righteous forsaken or his descendants begging bread"* (Psalm 37:25). Even in the midst of the Great Recession the children of God who walk uncompromisingly before Him will not be forsaken and we certainly won't have to beg for a crust of bed. We shall lend and not have to borrow. David went on to say in verse 26 that *all day long he is gracious and lends, And his descendants are a blessing.* David is telling us that because we are the righteous seed we are blessed, our descendants are blessed and we will always have the provisions to be a blessing. We must decide whether we want to walk in the blessings of the Lord or the curses of a sin sick people. Either way the choice is ours.

The Great Recession is far reaching and I believe that we all will feel the pains of its sting because God wants us to be aware of the conditions we are in. Even billionaires like Bill Gates and Warren Buffet have felt the erosive pains of our current economic system.

Know that God's people are not forsaken. His seed will not beg bread. We will have to walk through this horrendous recession, but we don't have to participate in it if we are faithful stewards of all that is entrusted to us. That doesn't mean hoarding every penny we lay our hands on. It doesn't mean becoming Mister or Miss Super Stingy either. James 5:1-6 gives this assessment of the hoarder or super stingy mindset, *"Come now, you rich, weep and howl for your miseries which are coming upon you. Your riches have rotted and your garments have become moth-eaten. Your gold and your silver have rusted; and their rust will be a witness against you and will consume your flesh like fire. It is in the last days that you have stored up your treasure! Behold, the pay of the laborers who mowed your fields, and which has been withheld by you, cries out against you; and the outcry of those who did the harvesting has reached the ears of the Lord of Sabaoth. You have lived luxuriously on the earth and led a life of wanton pleasure; you have fattened your hearts in a day of slaughter. You have condemned and put to death the righteous man; he does not resist you."*

What a cry from the Lord! Don't allow the spirit of greed to cause you, *"to store up your treasure and live luxuriously on the earth and lead a life of wanton pleasure while you condemn and put to death the righteous people around you."*

There's no denying it - we are in a recession, but as children of the Most High God, we can ride through the economic storm in such a way that it gives God glory. In ways that cause the world to look at "the church" and say, "how are they surviving? How is it that they are prospering in this time of economic trouble? As the wealth of our nation disintegrates under the weight of governmental and corporate corruption, it is time that the Church of Jesus Christ stand and take her place as a people that are righteous, holy and acceptable to God.

As the end times approaches, as people of God we must be able to stand and withstand the insurmountable pressures from the doctrines of man and the rudiments of this world. It is the doctrines and rudiments that have take this nation on a rollercoaster ride into economic devastation.

It is the hand of God that will bring us through. Even if this recession ends in 2012, what measures are in place to keep it from happening again? It is important to realize that this is a door that Satan will use to usher in his master deceiver, his CEO - the antichrist.

We must stand as the Church in unity if we are to overcome our current situation. The Lord said during prayer, *"until unity comes to leadership the people will continue to be divided."*

There's A Famine in the Land

We must come together in every area of life: socially, culturally, economically and spiritually if we are to bring unity to a dying world. The world MUST see the light of Jesus Christ through us. If the people who are called by the name of God would humble ourselves and pray, seek His face and turn from our wick ways, then He will hear from heaven, forgive our sin and heal our land.

We can continue to walk in faith, live in love and trust in God. We can be victorious in the midst of this calamity if we put our hope in God. Psalm 42 says, *"Put your hope in God, for I will yet praise him, my Savior and my God."*

Yes, there is a famine in the land, but we can show the world how to overcome. Our testimonies will show a dying world that Jesus is alive and working on behalf of those that are His. Remember, the righteous are not forsaken and His seed does not beg for bread. There is a famine in the land.

There's A Famine in the Land

Chapter 7

A Nation that Will Not Hear

"Behold, days are coming," declares the Lord GOD, "When I will send a famine on the land, Not a famine for bread or a thirst for water, But rather for hearing the words of the LORD.

Amos 8:11

Like the children of Israel, our nation repeatedly rejects the word of the Lord that is spoken through His Holy Bible and His true prophets. We are receiving what the world wants, to be left alone to be governed by the ungodly (*give us a king, we want a king*). Given over to organizations such as: the ACLU that attempts to set policies and laws through threats and coercion; Planned Parenthood kills the unborn; and a handful of anti-Christians that try to remove Christ from every area of our government, schools, etc.

The next time we find ourselves in the midst of another September 11th and we go running to God for guidance and deliverance - will He answer? No judgment is worse than silence from God. When September 11th occurred government officials prayed on the steps of our nation's capital. What happened? We got comfortable again and forgot about God.

Nothing will be more devastating than God turning this nation over to her sinful desires - her lusts, degradation, greed and perversions. The result, our nation becomes a slave to the godless countries we are in debt to.

There's A Famine in the Land

Note: Although most of the countries we are indebted to have trade agreements that keep their respective economies flowing, once the anti-Christ is on the scene, he won't show concern for the economic health of the United States. His concern will be world domination and the downfall of the United States will play a pivotal role in his master deception.

What can we do? If My people will…

1. Humble ourselves as a people and as a nation.

2. Pray

3. Seek the face of God.

4. Turn from our wickedness.

5. Keep our hearts and minds set on God.

There's A Famine in the Land

Chapter 8

Keep Your Heart Set on God...

The famine\recession is here and there is nothing we can do to stop it, but we can fast, pray, and trust God to bring us through it. We can do this by following these steps:

➢ Put your hope in God

➢ Commit your life to God

➢ Believe God and Believe in God.

➢ Walk each day in love for God and His people.

Put your hope in God, He is the **WAY** to survive the economic tsunami. He knows the **TRUTH** about everything that is ahead for us as a people,

77

as a nation and as the world. He is the **LIFE** that we must trust to bring us through. Jesus said: *"The thief comes only to steal and kill and destroy; I came that they may have life, and have it abundantly."* In other words, The **great recession** comes only to steal and kill and destroy; **Jesus** came that we may have life, and have life abundantly.

Walk out of this recession in abundance: financially, physically, spiritually and emotionally - knowing that it was the Lord who brought you out. He is bringing us out and He will rebuke the devourer for our sake.

Chapter 9

He Will Rebuke the Devourer

...I will rebuke the devourer for your sakes, and he shall not destroy the fruits of your ground; neither shall your vine cast her fruit before the time in the field, saith the LORD of hosts (Malachi 3:10-11 emphasis added).

To devour means "to eat up" "to consume." The enemy is devouring the seed of the United States, the church and even some of our homes.

Our decadence (immorality) and spiritual apathy (spiritual emptiness) has caused us to travel down a road of self destruction. We are seeing destruction in our finances, families, government and churches. We have been given over to the *"spirit of the seed eater"* who is eating away at our nation, our schools, and churches and in some cases our lives. We must give the reigns of our lives to the Lord Jehovah Jireh, our source and provider.

"But it shall come about, if you do not obey the LORD your God, to observe to do all His commandments and His statutes with which I charge you today, that all these curses will come upon you and overtake you" (Deuteronomy 28:15). **Are we as a nation obeying the Lord?**

"The LORD will send upon you curses, confusion, and rebuke, in all you undertake to do, until you are destroyed and until you perish quickly, on account of the evil of your deeds, because you have forsaken Me" (Deuteronomy

28:20). **Have we turned from our wicked ways? As a nation do you see curses of poverty, abuse, addictions, suicide and running rampant?**

"So all these curses shall come on you and pursue you and overtake you until you are destroyed, because you would not obey the LORD your God by keeping His commandments and His statutes which He commanded you" (Deuteronomy 28:45). **Has financial greed overtaken us? Has idolatry overtaken us? Have atrocities around the world overtaken us? Has spiritual wickedness set up strongholds in our churches?**

When we set our hearts on God, the enemy will not destroy the fruits of your ground; neither will you abort or miscarry your seed before the appointed time, says the LORD of hosts. If we want restoration in our homes, families, business or ministry, government or churches we must turn our hearts back to God.

The devourer is a dangerous spirit and he is eating away at the very fabric of our society. The devourer has eaten away at morality, decency, finances, compassion and more. It is going to take the heart of God to restore what the enemy has devoured.

Consecrate a fast, Proclaim a solemn assembly; Gather the elders And all the inhabitants of the land to the house of the LORD your God, And cry out to the LORD. Alas for the day! For the day of the LORD is near, And it will come as destruction from the Almighty. Has not food been cut off

There's A Famine in the Land

before our eyes (JOEL 1:14-16).

As a nation, we need to consecrate ourselves, proclaim an assembly of the people and come into the presence of the Lord with fasting, prayer and in submission to the Lord. Why? Because the day of the Lord is near and with it destruction, and famine. A famine for food and the word of God.

Take courage all is not lost. The Lord has issued a mandate to return to Him. He is saying, *"If my people, who are called by my name, will humble themselves and pray and seek my face and turn from their wicked ways, then will I hear from heaven and will forgive their sin and will heal their land. Now my eyes will be open and my ears attentive to the prayers offered in this place."* Therefore, *"Be glad in the LORD your God; For*

There's A Famine in the Land

He has given you the early rain for your vindication. And He has poured down for you the rain, The early and latter rain as before. The threshing floors will be full of grain, And the vats will overflow with the new wine and oil. "Then I will make up to you for the years That the swarming locust has eaten, The creeping locust, the stripping locust and the gnawing locust, My great army which I sent among you. "You will have plenty to eat and be satisfied And praise the name of the LORD your God, Who has dealt wondrously with you; Then My people will never be put to shame" (2 Chronicles 7:14 and Joel2:23-26, respectively). The Lord wants to rain on our economy, our families, our schools, our government and our churches. If we would allow the Lord to REIGN IN our lives, then He will RAIN ON our lives.

There's A Famine in the Land

There is a famine in the land, but as children of the Most High, we don't have to participate in its devastating effects. Be strong in the Lord and in the power of His might to bring us through the recession. Know that God is working this out for our good and His glory. As people of inheritance, God will shift us into position to receive the wealth that is laid up for us, but we must be in spiritual position to receive it. We can and will survive the "great recession" and we will do it by His Spirit reigning over us. STAND FIRM.

There's A Famine in the Land

There's A Famine in the Land

There's A Famine in the Land

About the Author

God has called Jacquie Hadnot to encourage, inspire, motivate and activate the gifts of the Spirit in order to raise powerful ministries in the body of Christ. She is becoming a voice on the subject of prayer, worship and spiritual warfare.

She is recognized as a modern-day apostle with a strong prophetic and psalmist anointing. She has a revelational teaching ministry with a mandate to saturate the world with the Word of God. Jacquie's heart is to see people arise and walk in the destiny and inheritance of the Lord.

She has founded and established It Is Written Ministries, a publication company, an accounting and consulting firm, and a global radio station. As a retired accountant and financial executive,

Jacquie blends ministerial and entrepreneurial applications in her ministry to enrich and empower a diverse audience with skills and abilities to take kingdoms for the Lord Jesus Christ. A lecturer, conference speaker, teacher, business trainer, and financial consultant, she provides consulting services to businesses, churches, and individuals. She has written over twenty-five books, manuals, and other materials on intimacy with God, prayer, fasting and spiritual warfare. She has also released several music Cds and received numerous music and book publishing awards.

Beyond the pulpit, Jacquie is a talk-show host on both television and radio with her own program,

Light for Your Path. Weekly she applies God's

wisdom to today's world solutions. Her ministry goal is to make Christ's teachings relevant for today. She also publishes a quarterly magazine by the same name.

In addition to her vast experience, Jacquie has a Th.d. in Pastoral Theology and a M.min. in Ministry Leadership. She is also a wife, mother of one daughter and grandmother of one grandson. She and her husband, Gregory presently pastor It Is Written Ministries in Kansas City Kansas. They also serve as owners and corporate officers of Igniting the Fire Media Group

There's A Famine in the Land

Other Books & Materials by Dr. Jacquie

~~~~~~~~~~~~~~~~~~~~~~~~~~~~~~~~~~~~

Books in Print
➢ Closing the Doors to Satan's Attacks: *Overcoming Fear*

➢ Trapped in the Arms of Death: *Overcoming Grip of Suicide*

➢ The Extravagant Love of God: Experiencing the Prophetic Flow

➢ Cry Aloud, Spare Not! A Prophetic Call to the Fast God Has Chosen

➢ Cry Aloud, Spare Not! The Companion-Study Guide

➢ His Mercy Endures Forever: Psalms, Prayers & Meditations

➢ To Make War with the Saints; Satan's Kingdom Agenda

➢ A Treasure in the Pleasure of Loving God

➢ Loving God through His Names: 365 Days of the Year

➢ Where Is Your God? Have We Lost the Referential Fear of the Lord?

Booklets
➢ When Fear Crept In

➢ Deeper…

➢ Naked, Broken and Unashamed

Audio Books & Teachings
➢ More of You… (Volume 1)

➢ In the Face of Adversity: *Overcoming Life's Storms*

There's A Famine in the Land

- Be Not Deceived…
- Where Is Your God?
- Recognizing Your Due Season
- Praying the Healing Scriptures
- The Enemy in Me: *Overcoming Self-Life Issues*

- Trusting God in a Season of Discouragement
- The Harlot Heart

Music
- The Extravagant Love of God
- The Spoken Word of Love
- His Mercy Endures Forever: Praying the Psalms

DVD
- When Your Faith is Being Tested
- What Made David Run
- Agents of Change
- Virtuous Women of Worship

TO CONTACE DR. JACQUIE:

www.jacquiehadnot.com
www.ignitingthefire.net
Or write us:
jacquie@jacquiehadnot.com

There's A Famine in the Land